# The Man in the Moon
## AND OTHER MOON TALES

## by Deborah Akers

HOUGHTON MIFFLIN     BOSTON

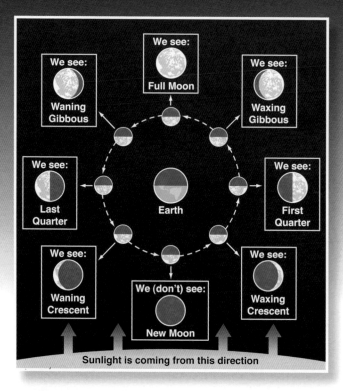

**A diagram of the Moon's path around Earth**

Almost every night, we can look out and see the Moon. And yet, every night it looks different. We call this the phases of the Moon. The Moon doesn't really change shape. It is always shaped like a ball. Why does the Moon look different?

**After a new moon, the Moon is seen in the night sky as a slim crescent.**

Every 27 and 1/3 days, the Moon completes one full path around Earth. The Moon also spins as it makes its orbit, or path, around Earth. The same side of the Moon always faces Earth. It is just that sometimes we can see more of it.

**Like Earth, the Moon makes no light of its own.**

The Moon does not make its own light. The light comes from the Sun. The Moon reflects the light from the Sun. As the Moon revolves around Earth, you see different amounts of the Moon's bright side. This causes the phases of the Moon.

**It may look like Swiss cheese, but the Moon is made of rock.**

Some days we cannot see the Moon at all. Some days we just see a thin sliver. Have you ever heard that the Moon is made of cheese? This story may have come from people looking at the half-full Moon. The Moon is really made of rock, not cheese.

**The harvest moon is the full moon that is closest to the date when fall begins.**

When it is a full moon, you can see by the light of the Moon. In the fall, the full moon starts to rise just as the Sun sets. This gives us extra light to do things outdoors. Farmers call this the harvest moon. They could use its light to finish harvesting crops.

**From Earth, only one side of the Moon can be seen.**

When the Moon is full, we can see all of its bright side. There are mountains, flat plains, and craters on the Moon. Many cultures tell stories of a "man in the moon." Can you see a face? These are really craters, or deep holes.

**Astronaut Edwin Aldrin stands by the United States flag on the Moon.**

People have always been interested in the Moon. Why does it change its shape? What is it like there?

Now we have traveled to the Moon. We have answers to some of our questions. But the Moon still makes us wonder as it moves across the night sky.

**Think About What You Have Read**

**1** Why does the Moon have phases?

**2** What is a harvest moon?

**3** Why do you think people are so interested in the Moon?

**Activity**

What would it be like to go to the Moon? Write about or draw what you imagine you would find if you traveled to the Moon.

# Earth Science: Patterns and Cycles on Earth and Beyond

ISBN-13: 978-0-618-59840-3
ISBN-10: 0-618-59840-5

90000>

9 780618 598403

HOUGHTON MIFFLIN

1-63363

# Still Standing

by Barbara Gannett

Number of Words: 388

ISBN-13: 978-0-618-59838-0
ISBN-10: 0-618-59838-3

3 4 5 6 7 8 9 SDP 14 13 12 11 10 09 08 07 06